Think Rich
Enjoy Riches

Think Rich
Enjoy Riches

ISBN 1453884319

First Published 2010

INTRODUCTION

*"Whatever you can do, or dream you can, begin it.
Boldness has genius, power, and magic in it."*
Goethe

The most successful people sustain a burning desire that upholds an unwavering purpose. When this condition is maintained, fulfillment unfolds in a natural and inexorable progression.

This book shows you exactly how to develop your own persistent, burning desire and then coaches you to the point where you are radically successful.

Can you develop a persistent burning desire?

The answer is a definite YES!

Imagine for a moment that a wealthy patron just proved to you, legal paperwork and all, that he put aside 10 million dollars for you in a trust fund that would become available to you at a randomly selected time within the next 2 years.
When pressed to tell you the exact date, he coyly reminds you that the paperwork says it is 100% for

sure, that you will definitely receive your $10 million, but that it could be at any time within two years. It could be in the next five minutes or it could be on the very last minute of the very last day.

Think for a moment about that fund. If you are like most people you will start to dream about all the great things you can do with the money. You will imagine how much better your life could be. You imagine the activities you would love to do. Soon you will feel a persistent burning desire to get at that fund. This burning desire may keep you up at night, thinking and dreaming about it.

You will begin to feel something akin to impatience and get a restless urge to do something to help speed it along. You may even ask your patron if there is something, anything, you can do to make the fund become available earlier.

From this scenario we learn:

1) Determining a very desirable result to hold in mind is the first step to achieving the outcome.
2) Believing that you will achieve the desirable result is the next step.
3) Once you believe that you will have what you desire you naturally begin to imagine all the

ways that the desirable result will improve
your life.

4) The visualized dreams of a better life ignite a
burning desire that motivates you to take
action to speed up the arrival of the result.

5) The persistent burning desire makes you think
of creative ways to facilitate the process. You
will begin to make plans of action.

6) You will begin to take steps that bring you
closer to your desired result.

7) Motivation plus the utilization of creativity
thus brings results much like a self-fulfilling
prophecy.

8) All of these things happen in a natural and
inexorable progression once you have
determined your goal and believe in the
undeniable realization of what you desire.

We have discovered that the first step to success is
to determine a very desirable result to hold in mind.
To achieve this step most effectively we use a
procedure to reveal your own personal and often
highly idiosyncratic areas of interest.

Once you recognize and resonate with your areas of
interest we will help you to develop your persistent
burning desire, easily and in a manner that comes
naturally. When you attain a persistent burning
desire with unwavering purpose you will surely

achieve what you seek. This is especially true when you use this book as your guide.

Let us now begin, together to uncover and manifest your deepest desires.

PART I

"To know thyself is the beginning of wisdom."
Socrates

One of the fastest ways to gain a clearer understanding of your areas of interest is for you to rate how well a series of carefully selected statements relate to you personally. The goal of this "Personality Probe" is not to define your personality, but to explore your preferences in order to help you find areas of interest sufficiently desirable as to excite a burning desire for them.

You are about to perform a distillation process whereby the essence of your life will be revealed.

In the back of the book there are Personality Probe Forms to fill out. You will find the numbers of the questions, Q1 through Q24, corresponding to the 24 statements below. You are going to write a numerical rating beside each of these numbers, to keep track of how strongly the statements apply to you.

Read the following statements and rate how strongly they apply to you. Zero means the statement does not apply to you at all. The number, 5, means that the statement matches you perfectly. Use intermediate numbers 1 to 4 to provide a measure of how strongly you agree that the statement is true for you. I'll show you how to interpret the results after you finish rating the statements.

1) You would rather read a good book than go to a good party if forced to choose.

2) At a dinner party you would rather have exactly your favorite food than share what the others are having.

3) At a social gathering you would rather sit near the edge of a room than in the center.

4) You would rather speak to a small group of acquaintances than a large group of acquaintances.

5) You would rather follow a proven method than find a better way yourself.

6) Day by day you think about what is happening more than what could happen or could have happened.

7) You most often do things the way they are supposed to be done rather than exploring and improvising.

8) You like tidying up and arranging rather than thinking about future scenarios.

9) You prefer books with exciting theories instead of ones with engaging fiction.

10) You make decisions based much more on reasoning than on feeling.

11) You like to plan your actions and are not very often swayed by your emotions.

12) You have difficulty expressing your deepest feelings.

13) You like to make lists so that you can check off what you do during the day.

14) It is 3 a.m. (middle of the night), no cars are coming in any direction and no one is watching. You would wait at a long RED stoplight and would **NOT** go through it until it turned Green.

15) You evaluate things and situations according to criteria rather than accept and appreciate them as they are.

16) You just ate at a restaurant that received a bad rating although the food you ate was very satisfying. You would **NOT** recommend this restaurant to a friend.

17) You enjoy spending your time helping people in need.

18) At a party you are always trying to make sure that everyone is enjoying themselves.

19) If you were on an outing with friends and you found 100 dollars in small bills you would find more satisfaction sharing the money than you would discretely keeping it for yourself.

20) A company you work for offers to increase your salary by half the salary of anyone you lay off. You would **not** lay anyone off.

21) You would rather plan all your activities in advance than wait and make spontaneous decisions according to the perceived needs of the moment.

22) You are very happy going directly from one activity to another without needing time to ponder in between activities.

23) You would much rather ask someone to provide direction, rather than have to figure out what you should be doing all by yourself.

24) You like to have a full schedule of activities so that you do not have to figure out how to occupy yourself.

Now you have answered each of the 24 questions and have put a numerical rating beside each of them. To derive your particular areas of interest, you will need to add up your answers in the following way.

Divide the questions into groups of four. Take your rating for the questions 1 through 4, and add them together. Now subtract 10, and you will have your final answer for this first group of 4 questions.

My rating for the first group of four questions was:

1) 3
2) 5
3) 3
4) 3

Following the procedure above, I add the ratings together to produce the number 14. (3+5+3+3=14) Then I subtract 10 from 14 to produce the number 4.

Four is my final numerical result for this first group of 4 questions.

My rating for the second group of four questions was:

5) 0
6) 2
7) 1
8) 0

Following the procedure above, I add the ratings together to produce the number 3. (0+2+1+0=3) Then I subtract 10 from 3 to produce the number -7. Minus 7 is my final numerical result for this second group of 4 questions. Notice that this second number was negative. The results can be Negative or Positive.

You will follow this procedure for the entire six groups of 4 questions. Once this is done you will end up with six final numbers that will be used to highlight your areas of interest.

Let me remind you to fill out the Personality Probe Form at the end of this book.

We use the six personality dipoles listed below to isolate your own personal areas of interest.

Keep in mind that by this process, we are pinpointing areas of particular interest to you so that you will develop a persistent burning desire, upholding an unwavering purpose. Once this is achieved, and with appropriate coaching such as provided herein, success unfolds in an inexorable fashion.

PERSONALITY DIPOLES:

Extrovert and Introvert

Intuitive and Sensing

Thinking and Feeling

Judging and Perceiving

Altruistic and Detached

Busy and Open

Extrovert (E): Favors the outer world of people and things. Extroversion involves interacting with people, having broad ranging interests, and tending to act first and think later.

Introvert (I): Favors the inner world of ideas and information. Introversion involves concentrating on a small number of deep issues, and thinking things through carefully before acting.

Sensing (S): Favors facts and tangible outcomes. A sensing person looks for facts and practical approaches, and is more interested in detailed and unambiguous information.

Intuitive (N): Favors possibilities and potential. Intuition looks at potential and future possibilities, and tends to be interested in making discoveries and in the future.

Thinking (T): Favors decisions based on analysis and critical thinking, often using objective logic to form a detached, objective view.

Feeling (F): Favors using values and feelings to form an appreciation of a person or situation.

Judging (J): Favors living a structured, organized and stable life. Tends to make evaluations by comparing against a predetermined set of criteria or metrics.

Perceptive (P): Favors living flexibly and going with the flow by attending to what is happening in the present moment. Tends to accept each situation according to its own specific and perhaps even unique attributes.

Altruistic (A): Finds fulfillment in serving others and in making a personal connection through the act of giving. Tends to place a lot of emphasis on the wellbeing of others.

Detached (D): Favors maintaining some distance between the self and other people. Does not need to make a human connection through daily activities in order to find fulfillment.

Busy (B): Does not mind having time tightly structured by other people. Is happy having a full schedule of activities without needing to have free time for the self. Perhaps even craves to have their time organized by others so that they know what they should be doing.

Open (O): Places a high value on having unstructured time available to be arranged at ones own discretion. Cherishes personal freedom, and freedom of choice minute by minute. Prefers to figure out what they should be doing for themselves and may resent being told what to do.

Determining your Results:

Your final answer for the first group of four
questions determines whether you are
Extrovert or Introvert
A negative result suggests that you are E
A positive number suggests you are I

The degree that you are either E or I is determined
by your numerical result, so that if you are a
-10, you are highly extroverted, +10 is highly
introverted, and zero can swing both ways.
This scale is used to determine each of the six group
ratings.

Likewise, your ratings for questions 5 through 8,
determines where you are on the scale from
Intuitive to Sensing. A negative result from 0 to
-10 determines how strongly you are Intuitive,
which is represented by the letter N. A positive
number suggests you are a Sensing person, which is
represented by the letter S

The ratings for questions 9 to 12 determine
Thinking or Feeling
A negative result suggests that you are an F
A positive number suggests you are a T

The ratings for questions 13 to 16 determine
Judging or Perceiving

A negative result = P
A positive number = J

The ratings for questions 17 to 20 determine
Altruistic and Detached
A negative result = D
A positive number = A

And finally, the ratings for questions 21 to 24
determine Busy or Open
A negative result = O
A positive = B

An example of a result would be **ESTJDB**.
The way you rated the statements would then
indicate that you have qualities that may be
described as: Extroverted, Sensing, Thinking,
Judging, Detached and Busy.

To make it easier to find your type we determine
your first four letters as defined by the first four
categories of the six bipolar characteristics.
For example, **ESTJ**:

Once you locate your first 4 letters, in this case
ESTJ, then look within this category to find your
last 2 bipolar characteristics, for example, **DB**.
These last two characteristics will define your areas
of interest for you.

Each of the 16 personality types are shown below, and each of these have 4 subgroups for a total of 64 types.

Each personality type has associated with it many path choices corresponding to areas of interest that will provide satisfaction for this personality type.

Within each category, I have also included **unfavorable** path choices that are unlikely to provide satisfaction for each of the 16 specific personality types. Look carefully at these areas corresponding to your type and verify that most if not all of these are indeed unattractive to you. You are well advised to avoid pursuing these areas if at all possible.

What is your personality type? Please locate it from the list below.

1) ISTJ => The Duty Fulfiller Examiner

ISTJ are perseverant. ISTJ will do anything that they have decided on. ISTJ will excel in a path in which they can use their excellent organizational skills and their powers of concentration to create order and structure. ISTJ fit extremely well into the Management and Executive layer of the corporate business world. Indeed, it is usually the ISTJ that build the corporate structures and it is they who make the rules that favor their advancement.

The following list of professions is built on our impressions of paths that would be especially suitable for an ISTJ. This is meant to be a starting place, rather than an exhaustive list. There are no guarantees that any or all of the paths listed here would be appropriate for you, or that your best path match is among those listed.

AO: search and rescue, fire fighter

DO: freelance accountant, mortician, tour guide

AB: high school teacher, search and rescue & trainer, fire fighter & trainer, martial arts instructor, fire chief, security professional

DB: bank examiners, auditors, corporate accountant, or tax examiners, legal counsel, military officer, librarian, data analyst, scientist, researcher, engineer, financial planner, statistician, office worker, government employee, lab technician, nuclear engineer, office manager, biomedical engineer, account manager, CEO, investment banker, analyst, academic, systems analyst, pharmacy technician, network admin, genetics researcher, research assistant, strategist

Unfavorable Paths: model, entertainer, music journalist, comedian, massage therapist, dj, author, bartender, painter, school counselor, artist, filmmaker, musician, actor, fashion desinger, singer, photographer

2) ISFJ=> The Nurturer Defender

ISFJ are very interested and in-tune with what other people are feeling. Yet they enjoy creating structure and order. Ideally, the ISFJ will choose a path in which they can use their exceptional people-observation skills to determine what people want or need, and then use their excellent organizational abilities to create a structured plan or environment for achieving what people want. They have an excellent sense of space and function, which combined with their aesthetic sensitivity, provides them special abilities in practical artistic endeavors, such as interior decorating and clothing design.

The following list of professions is built on our impressions of paths that would be especially suitable for an ISFJ. This is meant to be a starting place, rather than an exhaustive list. There are no guarantees that any or all of the paths listed here would be appropriate for you, or that your best path match is among those listed.

AO: early childhood development, social work/counselor, homemaker, stay at home parent, church worker.

DO: interior decorators, designers

AB: nurse, child care, health care worker, clergy

DB: administrators, administrative assistants
and office managers, paralegals, office worker,
personal assistant, school teacher, administrative
assistant, clerical employee, receptionist, library
assistant, dietitian, health educator, librarian

Unfavorable Paths: philosophy professor, bar
owner, comedian, dj, entertainer, psychotherapist,
bartender, entrepreneur, lecturer, astronomer, rock
star, filmmaker, performer, writer, ceo

3) INFJ => The Protector Theorist
INFJ is an individual who needs more than a mere
job. INFJ need to feel that what they choose to do is
in harmony with their deep sense of values and with
what they believe to be right. INFJ should choose a
path in which they live in a manner consistent with
their deeply held principles, and which supports
them in their quest to be engaged in meaningful
pursuits. INFJ possess a strong value system, and
persistent intuition along with a sense of "knowing".
They do best in positions in which they are leaders,
rather than followers. Although they can happily
follow individuals who are leading in a direction
that the INFJ fully supports, they will be very

unhappy following in any other situation.

The following list of professions is built on our impressions of paths that would be especially suitable for an INFJ. This is meant to be a starting place, rather than an exhaustive list. There are no guarantees that any or all of the paths listed here would be appropriate for you, or that your best path match is among those listed.

AO: counseling and social workers, clergy/religious work. reflexologist, path counselor, homemaker

DO: philosophy, archaeology, literature/writer, musician, artist, photographers, designer, entrepreneur, painter, educational consultant, marketer, professor, music therapist, freelance writer, poet

AB: teacher, public speaking, coaching, medical doctor/dentist, alternative health care practitioner, chiropractor, activist/journalist, psychiatrist, psychologist, psychiatrist, child care/early childhood development, human resources, actor, psychotherapist

DB: web design, journalism, systems analyst, art curator, bookstore owner, teacher (art, drama, english), library assistant, professor of english, novelist, book editor, copywriter, philosopher, environmentalist, bookseller, museum curator, opera singer, magazine editor, archivist, screenwriter, film director, creative director, librarian, social services worker, art historian, sign language interpreter, photo journalist, makeup artist

Unfavorable Paths: executive, lab technician, restaurant owner, strategist, ceo, bar owner, marketing specialist, business consultant, airline pilot, Stewardess, race car driver, businessman, information technology consultant, administrator, supervisor, bartender

4) INTJ => The Scientist/ Strategist

INTJ are brilliant at grasping complex theories and applying them to problems in order to achieve resolutions. This type of strategizing is the central focus and drive of the INTJ, hence there is a happy match between desire and ability. INTJ is happiest and most effective in paths that allow problem solving, and which support autonomy over their daily lives.

The following list of professions is built on our impressions of paths that would be especially suitable for an INTJ. It is meant to be a starting place, rather than an exhaustive list. There are no guarantees that any or all of the paths listed here would be appropriate for you, or that your best path match is among those listed.

AO: activist, find cures for rare diseases, prosthesis designer, problem solver consultant, urban planner, ecologist, inventor

DO: corporate strategists and organization builders, science writer, inventor

AB: professors and teachers, medical doctors/dentists, business administrators/managers

DB: scientists, engineers, military leaders, lawyers/attorneys, judges, computer programmers, systems analysts and computer specialists, biologist, inventor, forensic anthropologist, systems analyst, philosopher, nuclear engineer, political analyst, researcher, statistician, scholar, research scientist, computer scientist, software designer, curator, computer programmer, aerospace engineer, electrical engineer, paleontologist, mechanic, astronomer, fighter pilot, librarian, systems administrator, neurosurgeon, book editor, biotechnology, archeologist, lab tech, bookstore owner, english professor, philosophy professor, chemical engineer, epidemiologist, forensic scientist, museum curator, research assistant

Unfavorable Paths: performer, singer, art therapist, childcare worker, hair dresser, wedding planner, advertising executive, job in entertainment industry, bartender, dj, event coordinator

5) ISTP => The Vigilante Craftsman

ISTP have the abilities to be good at many different kinds of tasks. They are both introverted, and thinking. This gives them the ability to concentrate and work through problems which leaves many doors open to them. ISTP needs to lead a lifestyle that offers a great deal of autonomy and does not include too much external enforcement of structure. ISTP are happiest working for themselves, or working in very flexible environments. Their natural interests lean towards applying their excellent reasoning skills to integrate with known facts and data to discover underlying structure, or solutions to practical questions.

The following list of professions is built on our impressions of paths that would be especially suitable for an ISTP. This is meant to be a starting place, rather than an exhaustive list. There are no guarantees that any or all of the paths listed here would be appropriate for you, or that your best path match is among those listed.

AO: firefighter, paramedic/EMT

DO: business analyst, athlete, construction worker, carpenter, driver, detective, entrepreneur, farmer, motorcyclist, military, mechanic, pilot

AB: dental hygienist, human resources

DB: computer specialist, engineer, electrical engineer, forensic pathologist, marketer, project manager, police, probation officer, steelworker, systems analyst, technical specialist, aerospace engineer, software engineer, software developer, scientist, bar owner, automotive technician, electrician, engineer, mathematician, industrial engineer, nuclear engineer, biotechnology, mechanic, systems analyst, computer animator, data analyst, video game designer, technician, computer scientist

Unfavorable Paths: artist, fashion designer, theater director, poet, dancer, actor, singer, english teacher or professor, art teacher, healer, stage manager, florist, art therapist, school teacher, music journalist

6) ISFP => The Artist

ISFP need a meaningful path that is more than a job. The middle of the road is not likely to be a place where they will be fulfilled and happy. ISFP need a path consistent with their strong core of inner values. They live in the moment, and take the time to savor it. They do not do well in most fast-paced corporate environments. They need a great deal of autonomy so they can function in their natural realm of acute sensory awareness. Give freedom to explore they may find a wonderful artist within themselves. Almost every well-known artist in the world has been an ISFP. The ISFP is acutely aware of people's feelings and reactions, and is driven by their inner values to help people. This predisposes the ISFP to be a natural counselor and teacher.

The following list of professions is built on our impressions of paths that would be especially suitable for an ISFP. This is meant to be a starting place, rather than an exhaustive list. There are no guarantees that any or all of the paths listed here would be appropriate for you, or that your best path match is among those listed.

AO: church worker, naturalist, psychologist, physical therapist, homemaker, stay at home parent, pastor, humanitarian artist

DO: artist, composer, designer, forest ranger, librarian, musician, singer

AB: counselor, child care, medical staff, nurse, early childhood development, pediatrician

DB: administrative assistant, clerical supervisor, carpenter, chef, mechanic, dental staff, editor, sports management, school teacher, carpenter, veterinary technician, health educator, hospitality worker, athlete, physician assistant, photographer, health care worker, shop assistant, stylist, website designer, graphic artist, aesthetic real estate developer.

Unfavorable Paths: politician, actor, psychoanalyst, dj, judge, entrepreneur, attorney, professor, marketing, academic, criminal psychologist.

7) INFP => The Dreamer Idealist

INFP are sensitive individuals who need a path that is more than a job. INFP need to feel everything they do is in accordance with their strongly felt value system, and is moving them or others in a positive direction. INFP are driven to act with meaning and purpose. The INFP will be happiest when their daily lives are congruent with their values, and when they can work towards the greater good of humanity. Many great authors have been INFP.

The following list of professions is built on our impressions of paths that would be especially suitable for an INFP. This is meant to be a starting place, rather than an exhaustive list. There are no guarates that any or all of the paths listed here would be appropriate for you, or that your best path match is among those listed.

AO: activist, counselor, church worker, massage therapist, missionary, minister, physical therapist

DO: architect, artist, editor, filmmaker, fashion designer, graphic/web designer, holistic health practitioner, librarian, legal mediator, musician, photographer, writer, freelance artist

AB: employee development specialist, psychologist/counselor, speech pathologist, social worker, actor

DB: educational consultant, human resources, journalist, translator/interpreter, teacher/professor, video editor, poet, painter, art therapist, teacher (art, music, drama), songwriter, art historian, library assistant, composer, work in the performing arts, art curator, playwrite, bookseller, cartoonist, video editor, photographer, philosopher, record store owner, digital artist, cinematographer, costume designer, film producer, philosophy professor, librarian, music therapist, environmentalist, movie director, activist, bookstore owner, filmmaker

Unfavorable Paths: business owner, supervisor,

office manager, business analyst, ceo, executive assistant, judge, event coordinator, lawyer, office worker, business professional, manager, executive, administrator, financial analyst, public relations manager.

8) INTP => Engineer Nerd

INTP are gifted at generating and analyzing theories and possibilities to prove or disprove them. INTP have a great deal of insight and are creative thinkers, which allows them to quickly grasp complex abstract thoughts. They also have exceptional logical and rational reasoning skills that assist in the analysis of theories to discover the essence about them. INTP is driven to seek clarity in the world and thus enjoy a happy match between desire and ability. INTP are happiest in paths supporting autonomy in which they can work primarily alone on developing and analyzing complex theories and abstractions, with the goal of their work being the discovery of a truth, rather than the discovery of a practical application.

The following list of professions is built on our impressions of paths that would be especially suitable for an INTP. It is meant to be a starting place, rather than an exhaustive list. There are no guarantees that any or all of the paths listed here would be appropriate for you, or that your best path match is among those listed.

AO: designer of mechanisms and systems to help people or the environment, freelance medical, vocational scientist, architect of ideas, inventor

DO: consultant, forestry/park ranger, musician, philosopher, archeologist, computer repair, freelance science writer, philosophy professor, engineering consultant, inventor

AB: teacher/professor

DB: computer specialist, computer animator, computer programmer, engineer, economist, financial planner, investigator, investment banker, inventor, interpreter/translator, judge, legal mediator, logician, lawyer/attorney, mathematician, researcher, systems analyst, scientist, strategic planner, technical writer, science writer, game designer, scientist, software engineer, research scientist, physicist, software developer, geologist, computer scientist, philosophy professor, webmaster, medical researcher, systems analyst, comic book artist, computer technician, website designer, scholar, forensic anthropologist, astronaut, researcher, historian, systems engineer, genetics researcher, astronomer, environmental scientist, egyptologist

Unfavorable Paths: health care worker, trainer, school teacher, wedding planner, social worker, guidance counselor, supervisor, child care worker, fundraiser, customer service, stay at home parent, office administrator, movie star, hospitality worker, human resources, public relations

9) ESTP => The Persuader Marketer

ESTP enjoy advantageous traits that are unique to their personality type. Their skills of observation make them extremely good at astutely analyzing and assessing other peoples' motives or perspectives. Their people skills allow them to use knowledge gleaned to their advantage while interacting with people. For this reason, ESTP are excellent salespeople. They also have an exceptional ability to react quickly and appropriately to an immediate need, such as in an emergency or crisis situation. This is a valuable skill in many different professions, perhaps most notably in action-oriented professions, such as police work. ESTP enjoy new experiences and dealing with people, and dislike being confined in structured or regimented environments. They also want rapid feedback for their actions, and don't like dealing with a lot of high-level theory that would require delaying gratification. For these reasons, they should choose paths involving intensive interaction with people, and that do not require the performance of routine, detailed tasks.

The following list of professions is built on our impressions of paths that would be especially suitable for an ESTP. It is meant to be a starting place, rather than an exhaustive list. There are no guarantees that any or all of the paths listed here would be appropriate for you, or that your best path match is among those listed.

AO: firefighter, paramedic/EMT

DO: comedian, carpenter, driver, detective, entrepreneur, farmer, laborer

AB: personal coach, life counselor, fundraiser, personal fitness trainer.

DB: agent, auditor, computer technician, craftsman, computer tech support, engineer, police, sales representative, military, marketer, network specialist, project manager, CEO, sports management, fighter pilot, marketing specialist, business manager, race car driver, supervisor, economist, airline pilot, bar owner, consultant, cia agent, security specialist, technician, businessman, mechanical engineer, public relations specialist, coach, manager, marketing director, sales associate, mechanic, politician, publicist

Unfavorable Paths: college student, editor, philosopher, museum curator, librarian, freelance writer, author, florist, painter, school psychologist, poet, artist, art teacher, novelist, bookstore owner, graphics designer, songwriter, musician, professional english professor

10 ESFP => The Entertainer Performer

ESFP have a wide range of abilities but are happiest when they have a lot of contact with people, and are generating new experiences. They are best suited to situations that provide opportunities to use their people skills according to their practical nature. This relish challenges that allow them to stay engaged and interested.

The following list of professions is built on our impressions of paths that would be especially suitable for an ESFP. It is meant to be a starting place, rather than an exhaustive list. There are no guarantees that any or all of the paths listed here would be appropriate for you, or that your best path match is among those listed.

AO: church worker, personal trainer, massage therapist, physical therapist

DO: makeup artist, entrepreneur, musician, fashion designer, photographer

AB: child care, actor, school teacher

DB: administrative assistant, coach, comedian, lawyer/attorney, human resources, psychologist/counselor, recreation worker, receptionist, marketer, sales representative, social worker, public relations manager, radio dj, customer service, emt, hair stylist, event coordinator, pediatric nurse, public relations, human resources, travel agent

Unfavorable Paths philosophy professor, history professor, web developer, paleontologist, book editor, bookstore owner, author, researcher, painter, artist, scientist, cia agent, aerospace engineer, archeologist, webmaster, art director, computer programmer, freelance writer

11) ENFP => The Advocate Inspirer

ENFP excel at many different things, and therefore are able to achieve success in anything that interests them. ENFP become bored rather easily and are not gifted at following things through to completion. They should avoid jobs that require detailed, routine-oriented tasks, or positions that are confining and regimented. They will do best in professions that encourage them to creatively generate new ideas and deal closely with people.

The following list of professions is built on our impressions of paths that would be especially suitable for an ENFP. It is meant to be a starting place, rather than an exhaustive list. There are no guarantees that any or all of the paths listed here would be appropriate for you, or that your best path match is among those listed.

AO: church worker, homemaker, massage therapist, record store owner, some job related to theater/drama, poet, music journalist, freelance artist, entrepreneur with a mission to help people.

DO: artist, make up artist, entrepreneur, musician, painter, writer, performer, entertainer, songwriter, musician, filmmaker, comedian, singer, movie producer, playwright

AB: actor, path counselor, human resources, nurse, occupational therapist, psychologist/counselor, social worker, speech pathologist, teacher/professor, teacher (art, drama, music),

DB: art director, accountant/auditor, banker/economist, consultant, conference planner, diplomat, dietitian/nutritionist, designer, engineer, editor, housing director, journalist, lawyer/attorney, merchandise planner, marketer, newscaster, public relations, politician, project manager, social scientist, senior manager, trainer, technical specialist, radio broadcaster/dj, work in fashion industry, bartender, comic book author, work in television, dancer, artist, model, costume designer, choreographer,

Unfavorable Paths: office manager, mathematician, investment banker, office worker, computer tech, it professional, network engineer, data analyst, scientist, researcher, financial advisor, business analyst, strategist, govt employee

12) ENTP => The Originator Inventor

ENTP are generally good at anything that captures their interest. They are likely to be able to enjoy success in many different paths. ENTP will do well to choose professions that allow them a lot of personal freedom and scope where they can use their creativity to generate new ideas and solve problems. They will not be completely happy in regimented or confining professions.

The following list of professions is built on our impressions of paths that would be especially suitable for an ENTP. It is meant to be a starting place, rather than an exhaustive list. There are no guarantees that any or all of the paths listed here would be appropriate for you, or that your best path match is among those listed.

AO: inventor of medical devices to ease suffering and/or help the environment, documentary producer, entrepreneur with a mission to help people.

DO: artist, musician, writer, photographer, international spy, freelance writer, creative director, professional skateboarder,

AB: actor, psychologist, psychiatrist

DB: consultant, computer programmer, comedian, computer, analyst, designer, engineer, entrepreneur, inventor, journalist, lawyer/attorney, marketer, politician, systems analyst, sales representative, scientist, computer consultant tv producer, philosopher, comedian, music performer, it consultant, fighter pilot, politician, diplomat, entertainer, game designer, bar owner, strategist, news anchor, airline pilot, comic book artist, college professor, private detective, mechanical engineer, lecturer, ambassador, astronomer, research scientist, judge, web developer, scholar, fbi agent, cia agent, electrical engineer,

Unfavorable Paths: interior decorator, clerical employee, government employee, social worker hospitality worker, occupational therapist, home maker, personal assistant, wedding planner, travel agent, secretary, pre school teacher, copy editor, child care worker.

13) ESTJ => The Overseer Bureaucrat

ESTJs are flexible in the types of paths that they choose. They excel at many professions, because they put forth a tremendous amount of effort towards doing things the right way. Their natural drive to be in charge will cause them to gravitate toward leadership positions. They are best suited for jobs that entail creating structure and order.

The following list of professions is built on our impressions of paths that would be especially suitable for an ESTJ. It is meant to be a starting place, rather than an exhaustive list. There are no guarantees that any or all of the paths listed here would be appropriate for you, or that your best path match is among those listed.

AO: business, administrator for a nonprofit, co-op or charity

DO: detective, writer

AB: teacher/professor, nursing, humanitarian police, peace corp.

DB: accountant, auditor, business analyst, business, administrator, banker, computer specialist, engineer, economist, editor, financial officer, government worker, insurance agent, judge, librarian, lecturer, military leader, marketer, manager, administrator, police, researcher, senior manager, sales representative, scientist, technical, executive, ceo, supervisor, business consultant, strategist, financial planner, business person, office manager, public relations manager, international business specialist, business analyst, management consultant, operations manager, loan officer, lawyer, marketing, sports management, government employee, investment banker specialist, underwriter,

Unfavorable Paths: record store owner, camera operator, art curator, film editor, video game designer, photo journalist, travel writer, poet, artist, songwriter, musician, novelist, art therapist, theatre teacher, actor, art historian, music teacher

14) ESFJ => The Supporter Controller

The ESFJ are extremely organized and enjoy creating order, and they find satisfaction largely through giving and helping others. They thus do well at tasks that involve creating or maintaining order and structure, and they are happiest when they are serving others.

The following list of professions is built on our impressions of paths that would be especially suitable for an ESFJ. It is meant to be a starting place, rather than an exhaustive list. There are no guarantees that any or all of the paths listed here would be appropriate for you, or that your best path match is among those listed.

AO: family doctor, homemaker, church worker

DO: librarian, trainer, small business consultant, conference organizer, workshop organizer

AB: counselor, child care, nurse, speech pathologist, social worker, dental assistant, teacher, human resources, pediatrician, kindergarten teacher, security professional

DB: accountant, administrator, administrative assistant, bookkeeper, marketer, office manager, organization leader, researcher, radiological technologist, receptionist, wedding planner, public health employee, business consultant, human resources manager, executive assistant, public relations specialist, medical employee, office worker, social services

Unfavorable Paths: scientist, computer consultant, tattoo artist, game designer, philosophy professor, international spy, film director, artist, author, filmmaker, philosopher, video editor, musician, poet, astronaut, art curator, cartoonist, graphics designer

15) ENFJ => Mentor Guide

ENFJ enjoy a flexibility of characteristics that offers a wide scope in choosing a profession. They are likely to do very well as long as they're in a supportive environment where they have an opportunity to work with people and face sufficient diverse challenges to stimulate their creativity.

The following list of professions is built on our impressions of paths that would be especially suitable for an ENFJ. It is meant to be a starting place, rather than an exhaustive list. There are no guarantees that any or all of the paths listed here would be appropriate for you, or that your best path match is among those listed here.

AO: church worker, homemaker, facilitator

DO: artist, consultant, librarian, musician, film critic, architect

AB: actor, path counselor, teacher (art, preschool, elementary), facilitator, human resources, nurse, occupational therapist, psychiatrist, psychologist, counselor, school psychologist, childcare worker,

DB: accountant/auditor, administrator, administrative assistant, banker/economist, diplomat, designer, events coordinator, editor, project manager, politician, casting director, wedding planner, work in the performing arts, fashion designer, news anchor, fashion merchandiser, broadcaster, stylist, interior designer, restaurant owner, hair stylist, film director, dancer

Unfavorable Paths: business consultant, dj, bookseller, financial manager, epidemiologist, truck driver, electrical engineer, software designer, race car driver, scientist, computer specialist, airline pilot, computer programmer, web designer

16) ENTJ => Chief Overlord

ENTJ are especially endowed to be leaders and builders of organizations. They are quick to clearly identify problems and come up with innovative solutions for the short and long-term well being of an organization. Having a strong desire to lead, they're not likely to thrive as followers. ENTJ crave being in charge, and need to be in charge in order to capitalize on their special capabilities.

The following list of professions is built on our impressions of paths that would be especially suitable for an ENTJ. It is meant to be a starting place, rather than an exhaustive list. There are no guarantees that any or all of the paths listed here would be appropriate for you, or that your best path match is among those listed.

AO: leader in the government, leader of co-op or charity

DO: entrepreneur, bounty hunter,

AB: teacher/professor

DB: business administrator, corporate executive officer, computer consultant, judge, lawyer/attorney, mortgage banker, manager, politician, scientist, marketing specialist, government employee, lawyer, developer, political scientist, international relations specialist, software designer, systems analyst, business manager, entertainment lawyer, foreign service officer, strategist, project manager, advertising executive, cia agent, marketing manager, private investigator, administrator, business analyst, management consultant, film producer, financial advisor, cardiologist, professor, fbi agent

Unfavorable Paths: photographer, massage therapist, video editor, english professor, chef, health care worker, singer, bookstore owner, job in the performing arts, poet, child psychologist

PART II

"Tell me and I'll forget; show me and I may remember; involve me and I'll understand."
Chinese proverb

Now that you have highlighted some areas of interest to your particular personality preferences, I invite you to use what you have learned about your self by implementing some basic tools for unleashing your full potential. Narrowing down your areas of interest will undoubtedly reveal in you one persistent burning desire that will inspire an unwavering sense of purpose.

As an exercise, I'd like you to imagine what could have happened if the following famous people had been thrown off track but had been able to take the Personality Probe to develop a deeper understanding of their own character. You can then see how a deeper understanding would allow them to get back on track so that they would be able to achieve unprecedented success pursuing their deepest desires. You will see from the following examples how knowing oneself will help you avoid unfavorable choices, and bring you to a successful fulfillment of your life's purpose.

Example 1: Imagine that Bill Gates had rebelled against his father and had become a Child Psychologist, a path in which he became frustrated because it drained him emotionally. Imagine that he took the personality probe that you have just taken, and discovered that he is an **ENTJDB**. He finds the areas of interest listed for his personality type, and after pondering this list, several categories, (highlighted below), begin to generate a level of excitement in him and he starts dreaming about them.

DB: business administrator, **corporate executive officer, computer consultant**, judge, lawyer/attorney, mortgage banker, manager, politician, scientist, marketing specialist, government employee, lawyer, developer, political scientist, international relations specialist, **software designer,** systems analyst, business manager, entertainment lawyer, foreign service officer, **strategist**, **project manager**, advertising executive, cia agent, marketing manager, private investigator, administrator, business analyst, management consultant, film producer, financial advisor, cardiologist, professor, fbi agent

He then selects these top five areas of interest and lists them in order of intensity producing the following:

1. corporate executive officer
2. strategist
3. software designer
4. computer consultant
5. project manager

On examining this list he realizes that he would love to head up a software company that builds the most strategically important next generation of software applications. He is empowered in the knowledge that his personality type is a "Chief Overlord", and understands why he wants to dominate the new software industry.

The more he thinks about his new software company the more he desires its creation. He now feels a persistent burning desire upholding an unwavering sense of purpose that leads him to his single goal, and his personal success.

Example 2: Imagine that Oprah Winfrey got off to a wrong start by becoming a Flight Attendant, because she thought she would enjoy traveling and interacting with people. Unfortunately, she soon discovered that the level of interaction she received as a Flight Attendant was not deep enough, and intellectually she was hungry for something more stimulating. She read this book and took the questionnaire.

She found that her personality profile is that of an INFJA. She was split between O and B, because although she liked to be engaged with people (Busy) she needed to get away by herself to recharge (Open) every now and then.

She read through her interest areas and found that Flight Attendant was not a good path choice for her personality type. She pondered the more suitable interest areas including both INFJAB and INFJAO. It was as if a dam broke inside of her. She suddenly saw many areas that beckoned to her.

AO: <u>counseling and social workers</u>, clergy/religious work. reflexologist, **<u>path counselor</u>**, homemaker

AB: <u>teacher</u>, <u>public speaking</u>, <u>coaching</u>, medical doctor/dentist, alternative health care practitioner, chiropractor, psychologist**, <u>activist/journalist</u>**, psychiatrist, psychologist, psychiatrist, child care/early childhood development, human resources, **<u>actor</u>**, psychotherapist

Following the instructions she wrote out the 5 areas of most interest to her.

1. activist/journalist
2. counseling and social workers
3. public speaking/actor
4. path counselor
5. teacher/coaching

A pattern emerged where she could see herself in the media as someone who gets in close to people and helps them. She imagined how wonderful it would feel to be discussing issues that really mattered to people. She envisioned herself as a "Soft" journalist/public speaker/counselor, someone that the ordinary person could relate to. She began to look for issues of the "heart" that she could engage the public with.

The more she looked at the list of 5 items above the stronger became her desire. Soon she had lit a bonfire within her heart that gave her an unwavering sense of purpose.

Example 3: Imagine that Mother Teresa had started out as a writer. She wrote about spiritual matters and this was good as far as it went but she felt that she was missing something vital. She took our Personality Probe and discovered that her personality profile was ISFJA with a split between B and O. She liked to be busy but her spirituality required time on her own for prayer and meditation. She found out that a writer was not on the recommended path list for her personality type. Instead what was recommended for ISFJ was:

AO: <u>early childhood development</u>, <u>social work/counselor</u>, homemaker, stay at home parent, **<u>church worker</u>**.
interior decorators, designers

AB: <u>nurse</u>, <u>child care</u>, <u>health care worker</u>, <u>clergy</u>

When she pondered this list she began to feel an intense longing. She wrote down her areas of interest.

1. clergy
2. church worker
3. child (of God) care
4. nurse/health care worker
5. social work/counselor

She was overwhelmed by what she saw in the list. It was a revelation. She now knew beyond a doubt that she belonged in the church, working in the front lines, helping god's children, healing the sick when possible and reducing suffering where ever possible. She realized that God is manifest in people and that she could serve him best by taking care of people who are in the most profound state of need. From that point on Mother Teresa was consumed by her burning passion to serve. She was guided by an unwavering sense of purpose that showed her in no uncertain terms what needed to be done.

Now it is your turn to put the Personality Probe to work for you. Examine your own personality profile. Combine the path choices from both personality poles whenever the score is 2 or less, either plus or minus. For example, if you scored 1 as a **Thinker** (**T**), then also review the choices for your personality type for the **Feeling** (**F**) category. The reason is that your preference for thinking over feeling is not that strong and you are likely to oscillate in your preferences.

Think deeply about each of the corresponding path choices that match your personality type. Some will speak to your heart immediately, others you may choose to eliminate. Take your time reviewing each suggested path. Remember, if you have more borderline categories combine the path choices from both the personality poles of those as well.

Consolidate the path choices that apply to your type and highlight anything in the list that interests you. Review your choices, and narrow or expand your list of highlights to your TOP FIVE LIST, this will be what we call your TOPLIFE LIST.

There is a TOPLIFE LIST form at the Back of the book for you to fill out. Keep this list and refer to it from time to time while looking for patterns that are attractive to you.

Ponder this list and allow your imagination to play with it. Imagine something that you would love to do that may include one or more items from the list. Does this list remind you of anything you have longed for, or dreamed of, or "wanted to be when you grow up"?

Allow your openness of mind to dream your self into each of your toplife situations. Dreaming about each will allow you a glimpse of the possibilities available to you.

Keep your toplife list in a place where you can refer to it often. This list represents the distilled essence of your heart's desire. Very likely your future success and happiness is contained within this list. Some of you may see your ideal choice right away. Others may find that your hearts desire is revealed progressively as you begin to gain more belief in your power to manifest what you desire. We will revisit your toplife list many times so that you have ample opportunities to gain clarity. By pondering and dreaming about each of the toplife choices, you will begin to form a burning desire for some combination of these paths.

Contained within your toplife list is the substance of your life's purpose. To the untrained eye it is a list of jobs, but as you continue to put your attention on your toplife list, a pattern will emerge. It is not necessary to make your choice in haste. We will keep referring back to your toplife list with progressive clarity and you will discover the essence of your list, and how it relates to your life at this present moment, and for your future.

PART III

"For as he thinketh in his heart, so is he."
Proverbs 23:7

You have now created your toplife list. I invite you to write in a notebook, or in the notes section at the back of this book, some of the details of a life that you would consider ideal. Be sure to include as many sense or feeling words as possible in your description. The more specific you are with your words, the stronger your vision will be. Below are some sample questions to help activate your creativity and get it flowing:

Where are you living in your ideal situation?
What does your house look like; your furniture; your clothing?
What are you doing that you are really good at?
What would you love to be able to offer to the world?
How much money do you have available?
How much free time do you have?
How do you see yourself spending your time in an ideal situation?
What type of relationships have you cultivated with your family or friends or with your life partner?
How does it feel to move in your ideal body?

How are you growing as a person?
What values are you providing to your fellow men
and to the world?
What are you doing that brings you the most joy and
satisfaction?

Answer every question you conjure. The more
specific you are with your words, the more specific
your manifestation will be. As you write out your
scenarios, you will begin to feel a stirring of desire
within your being. Throughout this exercise it is
best not to limit yourself to what you think is
"realistic". As you will discover, reality is very
plastic and can be molded like clay in your hands.
Much better is to focus on creating ideal scenarios,
ones that are very attractive to you. Creating an
attractive ideal is the first step to success.

Holding an ideal in mind, empowered by belief in
the ideal, makes the desired results real in a way that
is very tangible. For me, this is like being on a lake
in a canoe. Our conscious mind is the paddle that
steers the canoe. Our paddles drive the canoe albeit
rather slowly. Our subconscious mind is a 50 hp
motor attached to the back of our canoe. This motor
drives our canoe effortlessly and at high speed.

Our conscious mind can be used like paddles to
point the canoe at a particular destination on the
shore on the other side of the lake. Imagine pointing

your canoe at the tallest pine tree on the far shore. As long as the paddles keep the nose of your canoe pointed at the largest pine tree the motor at the back will bring the tree closer and closer until your canoe arrives at its destination.

If at some point in the journey you lose concentration and the nose of your canoe is allowed to drift over to point at another destination, all is not lost. You have not lost all the progress you have made up until that point. The largest pine tree is still there as your destination point, and it is closer than it was originally. All that is required is for you to swing the nose of your canoe back over to your point of focus, your chosen destination, and you will resume your progress from the point at which you left off.

If you do not swing your canoe around, then you will move toward the other destination and away from the pine tree. So if you really wish to arrive at that pine tree, you certainly will arrive as long as you continue to point your canoe at your destination until you reach your destination. Just swing your canoe back on target as quickly as you can and you will soon be making progress again.

Your progress is incremental and is not easily lost. The pine tree is there whether you can see it or not. All you have to do is hold your destination firmly in mind as an ideal that you believe in. Use your conscious mind to steer your canoe and allow your subconscious to drive you there. Once you have a point of focus, hold fast to your destination, and all else will follow.

Along with the first stirrings of desire often come wafts of doubt that attempt to put out your fire. However, a proper understanding of the magnitude of human capabilities will dispel all your doubts, and will allow the fires of your desires to blaze. When you understand your true capabilities, which are astonishing, you will have the fervent belief that ignites a persistent burning desire and this necessarily brings about the desirable results you seek.

Each of us exists in an equilibrium established by our web of positive and negative thoughts. The more we think positive, plentiful and bountiful thoughts, the more capable we become.
It is our predominant thoughts that differentiate us from one another. It is our predominant thoughts that lift us to our success. Focus on the good in your life and you will grow the good. In so doing you are a conduit for ability; what I call a "CANDUIT".

The more we believe in our ability, the stronger becomes our burning desire for the result and the better we are able to marshal resources and take action to achieve it. More success leads to even greater belief in our ability to achieve the success we seek. We thus establish an empowering cycle that acts as a conduit for our ever, increasing ability. This is a CANDUIT® process.

A CANDUIT® is the opposite of a Catch-22 in that it opens up to greater freedoms and capabilities rather than trapping a person as does a Catch-22. Our socialization process imparts Catch-22 thinking to limit the people's power and to thus establish controls. As we learn to use the CANDUIT® process we expand our abilities and take back control over our thoughts, our lives and our destinies.

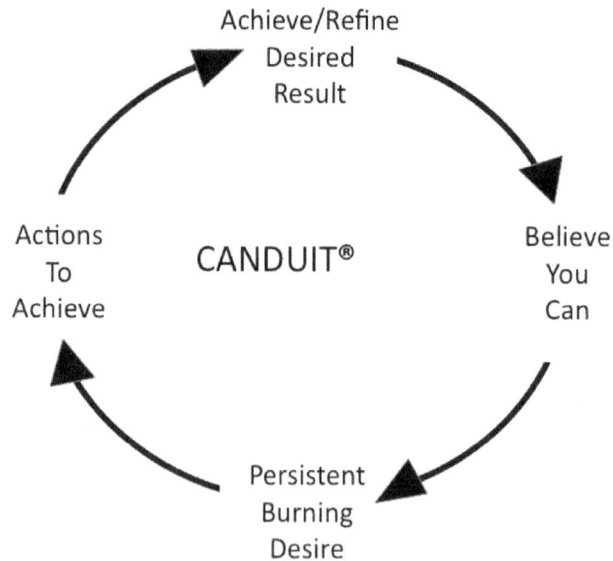

Our lives are the product of our predominant thoughts and emotions. Therefore the secret of all power, all achievement, and the accumulation of material goods, depends upon our method of thinking. What we are depends on how we think, and what we can do depends on what we are. Thus what we can do ultimately depends on our inner world of thought. The powers we possess are under our own control, because only we have control over our own thoughts.

Our thoughts create our reality and this is the source of all true power. This power does not need to be sought outside of your self. You already possess this power within your being and can use it to create an ideal life for yourself.

Let us explore further how our lives are a product of our thoughts. This fact has been amply demonstrated by scientific experiments.

For example, under hypnosis, people have accepted the suggestion that a wooden dowel is a hot poker. The suggestion actually manifests burn blisters on the skin. Belief in heat produced the same results as actual heat.

Do we consciously know how to create a burn blister without the application of heat, in the presence of belief? The answer is undoubtedly no, and yet we are able to do it anyway. Is there a scientist who can tell us in detail how a person can create the chemicals and the sequence of tissue changes leading up to the creation of a burn blister in the absence of heat but in the presence of belief? Again, the answer is no.

Belief allows the manifestation of abilities that we did not even know we had. Is there an ideal result you would like to manifest in your own life? Perhaps belief would help you to create this result.

Let me provide you another example. A doctor can administer an inert pill, a placebo, and tell the patient that it will soothe an ulcer. The stomach will then measurably secrete exactly the correct chemicals to soothe the ulcer and promote healing. Do we consciously know how to soothe an ulcer in the absence of true chemical agent? The answer is no but we do it anyway with sufficient belief.

No doctor can explain in scientific detail how our bodies can make exactly the correct chemicals on command to achieve these specific results. In its details this is a tremendous power. How it is accomplished is a complete mystery, and yet we do it and do it easily when we have sufficient belief.

Many people believe such feats to be impossible, yet we are faced with these occurrences on a daily basis. By such examples, and more, we come to know that thoughts, and belief in particular, are creative agents that are capable, with regularity, of manifestations that stagger the imagination.

We must now admit that marvelous feats are performed SUB-consciously. It is through the proper activation of the subconscious mind that we access vast constructive, and creative forces. The conclusion that you must now see is that every thought brings into action certain physical tissues, parts of brain, nerve, muscle or gland. Thoughts produce actual physical changes in the construction of the tissue. Therefore it is only necessary to entertain a sufficient number of thoughts on a given subject, in the presence of unwavering belief, to bring about a complete change in the physical organization of man.

Your external world is a reflection of your internal world. Harmony within thus translates to harmonious conditions in your world, agreeable surroundings, in short – the best of everything. Inner harmony imparts the ability to control our thoughts and to determine for ourselves how any experience affects us. Harmony experienced within leads to optimism and affluence, and it is thus that affluence within leads to affluence externally as well.

I invite you now to take a moment, either in your workbook, or in your creative imagination, to feel harmony and contentment. Take this moment to list every conceivable event, person or thing that you are grateful for in your life.

Success is a result. We create success by constructing an underlying foundation of causes for success. Every thought is a cause and every condition an effect of our thoughts. For this reason it is absolutely essential that we consciously channel our thoughts, consistently favoring the positive over the negative, so as to bring forth in our life, only desirable conditions.

Every thought is a choice for our highest good, and only we have the power to choose our thoughts. Whenever we wonder what others are thinking about us, we take our power outside our self and place it in the hands of another. Whenever we allow another to make a decision for us, regardless of the magnitude of that decision, we take our power outside our self, and put it in some one else's hands. Make your own choice, in thoughts and actions, and you will maintain the power to manifest your goals.

Thought concentrated on a highly desired purpose becomes all-powerful. Thought repeated becomes skill as it is delegated from the conscious mind to the vastly more efficacious subconscious mind. The human mind, if it is given a task that it perceives as difficult, looks for any excuse to shirk it. Most people tend to resist the idea of 'practice makes perfect'. If you had to think about each breath you take, how long could you sustain this practice?

Through repetition we are able to place our most important functions in the hands of a permanent and dependable power within us, our subconscious mind. The ease and perfection with which we achieve this power depends on the degree to which we can enlist our subconscious mind and cease to depend solely on the more limited conscious mind. The only task you have is to hold your ideal in your mind and keep it there. When you do this, coupled with your belief in the outcome, you will continue to move towards your ideal manifestation.

Our conscious mind deals with the impressions and objects of outward life. It discriminates and makes choices. We reason with our conscious mind and can develop this power to a high degree. The power of will is carried in the conscious mind and it is through this conscious free will that we make choices. Our conscious mind can make impressions on other minds including that of our own subconscious. In this way our conscious mind can carry out its primary role, which is to become the responsible ruler and guardian of our subconscious mind. By perfecting the relationship between our conscious and subconscious minds we perfect the conditions of our lives and become responsible custodians of our manifestations.

Allow your self to stand watch as a sentinel, guarding your subconscious mind. Seek empowerment over your own thoughts, while resisting the possible negative influence of others.

The conditions of fear, worry, poverty and disease dominate humankind due to false suggestions impressed on the subconscious mind by the conscious mind. Our conscious mind can rapidly reverse all this by engaging in vigilant protective action over our thought processes.

Our conscious mind is the parent or guardian of our subconscious mind. A good parent provides a supportive and positive environment for development. Likewise, an aware and enlightened conscious mind provides good stewardship for the subconscious mind, so that our literal, and profound powers can be responsibly unleashed into our external world.

Remember that a good parent is also kind and forgiving. You may find yourself going off track every now and then. Whenever this happens the solution is to get back on track as if nothing happened. Re-establish your focus by visualizing your ideal life. Hold this image in your mind and keep it there. When you catch yourself wandering then re-establish your focus. Occupy your mind with whatever you wish to achieve and nothing else.

Get back on track and occupy your mind with what you wish to achieve.

Our conscious mind makes an impression on our subconscious mind by visualizing a very desirable outcome as already manifest. The strength of the impression is governed by the strength of our belief in the outcome. Belief is an investment of energy made by our conscious mind. Belief is the swinging of the sledgehammer that makes the impression upon the subconscious. If you wish to make an impression you must swing a fortified hammer of belief.

Our subconscious mind is the attentive servant on call 24 hours a day. It operates on the impressions of our conscious mind without question and with great speed and efficiency. By plainly stating to our subconscious mind specific things to be accomplished, in the presence of belief, powerful forces are set in motion that lead to the result desired. Indeed, those who learn to trust their subconscious mind find that they have essentially infinite resources at their command. You have this power as well. Begin to trust your subconscious mind and you will discover the powerful and infinite resources at your command.

All of us begin the process of mastery of our own lives, having accepted a mixture of right and wrong suggestions producing mixed results accordingly. The surest way to correct our situation is to overcome the wrong suggestions by using a strong counter suggestion, frequently repeated, which our subconscious mind must then accept. Our persistent vigilance over our thoughts will manifest for us our persistent burning desire. Eventually new and healthy habits of thought emerge supporting a healthy and abundant life.

The neural energy of our subconscious mind is projected onto the solar plexus of our body. The solar plexus is a nerve concentration or center in the abdomen that is situated behind the stomach and in front of the aorta and the diaphragm and contains several ganglia distributing nerve fibers to the viscera. The fact that the nerve fibers enter the viscera explains why we often experience intuitions from our subconscious as gut feelings. Solar Plexus literally means the Sun Center of the body, and is as its name suggests, a blazing star of energy.

The energy radiating from our solar plexus connects to our personal body, in that it vitalizes, energizes and directs the functioning of our various body systems. Lesser known is the fact that our solar plexus also connects with the communal body, which can be thought of as a giant biofeedback loop with the rest of the universe. We know that when we make decisions and impress these upon our subconscious mind we make changes that not only affect our own future but also affect the future evolution of the rest of the universe. Think of how Thomas Edison's decision to perfect the electric generator not only was beneficial to his own personal existence but also was beneficial to the existence of the rest of humanity. Our thoughts thus create causes that permeate both the personal and communal realms.

Our solar plexus is an omnipotent center of energy because it is a point of contact with all of life and therefore accomplishes whatever it is directed to accomplish. Our conscious thought is properly the master of this energy center and determines the nature of our experiences. Thoughts of courage, power, confidence, and hope, when combined with belief, all transmute into experiences of pleasure and profit.

Beware! The one emotion that short circuits this energy center, thereby shutting down body systems and harming also the communal network, is fear. Fear is the tightness that you feel in the pit of your stomach, your solar plexus. It is the cloud that obscures the sun. We use our knowledge of personal power to overcome fear and to banish fear from our lives in every aspect. When you acknowledge and thus believe in your infinite power you also know that you have nothing to fear.

The person who feels power flowing through his center will demand much and receive the greater portion. He radiates courage, confidence and power. All that is required is that you concentrate on the object of your desire. When you concentrate you impress your subconscious. In this way you convert the subtle and invisible force of desire, in the presence of belief, into actual tangible, concrete manifestations in your external world.

Our subconscious mind has abilities vastly greater than our conscious mind. Your conscious mind then cannot then be expected to instruct, in detail, your subconscious mind in how it is to realize the goals you impress upon it. To do so would be to unduly limit the power available to you. It is far more effective to simply say what you desire without worrying about how it is to be accomplished.

Compare the faltering piano playing of someone nervously picking away at each note directed by conscious attention to the seamless beauty of the music that results when the person is relaxed and the music is handed over to subconscious, automatic processes.

Tension leads to unrest and counterproductive agitation of the mind. It produces worry, the destructive cousin of fear. Relaxation is an absolute necessity to allow the mental faculties to exercise the greatest freedom and to produce the best results.

A very powerful impression you can use to strengthen your will and to realize your power to accomplish is the statement, "I am what I will myself to be." We can all benefit by repeating this to ourselves until it becomes a habit. "I am what I will myself to be."

PART IV

"Imagination is more important than knowledge."
Einstein

Now I invite you to revisit your toplife list. Find a quiet place where you can contemplate the multitudinous opportunities available to you. Power comes from quiet repose and contemplation, where we can be still and think.

Begin your contemplation with the statement, "I am what I will myself to be." Thought is the first step in all accomplishment.

Imagine already having the results you desire. Know that your results are already formed in your mind like a gift and that all you have to do is unwrap them. The more clearly you visualize your results and believe in them, the more powerful becomes your desire. Your desire in turn leads to your action, which is like unwrapping the gift presented by your mind.

Let go of all thoughts of adversity. Let go of all feelings of conflict within your being. Let go of anything that can be construed to be negative in any way. Releasing negative thoughts and emotions releases you so that you are elevated in your mind, in your feelings, and also in your external reality.

When you release the negative and embrace the positive it is like changing the channel on your reality. You suddenly find yourself living in a better place. You select a better reality from all the possibilities that reality presents to us all. The choice is yours to make. You now consistently make a choice for your highest good that leads you to your ideal goal.

The universe is filled with energy that has not yet taken a physical form. We are each a channel through which this undifferentiated energy becomes defined through form. You are a physical manifestation of this energy. The quality and quantity this form takes is up to each of us. YOU choose the level of quality of your channel. One of the surest ways to attain success is seek to be of greatest service to mankind, to seek the channel of most activity where you can do the most good according to your natural gifts and inclinations.

For example, which can accomplish more, a small battery or a heavy wire? A small battery fills up and then can take no more energy. A heavy wire channels the energy and can accomplish a great deal of useful work. If you keep everything to yourself then you are like a small battery. You fill up and

then can take on no more. When you find an outlet
for your goods or services then you are like a heavy
wire through which energy can flow in tremendous
quantity. To act like a powerful conduit then you
must find ways to give. To be successful you must
find ways to give and provide value. The more we
give the more we get.

When we channel our attention towards an exciting
goal supported by a belief in the outcome, we create
a powerful concentration of energy that overcomes
any obstacle. Imagine a powerful laser cutting
through a thick metal plate as though it were butter
and you will have a good metaphor for the power of
concentration.

How do we develop the power of concentration?
We do so by practice. Choose a small task that will
take you closer to your cherished result. Take action
and accomplish it. Feel the surge of energy flowing
through you like the closing of an electric circuit.
Use this energy surge to help you accomplish the
next step. The resulting surge of energy will be even
greater. Each step taken provides more than enough
energy to take the next step. You see that realizing
your cherished goals really is like unwrapping a
present. You do not so much create the result as
release it by acting as a channel for energy to flow
through you.

We develop the power of concentration through practice and we practice by visualizing our goals and then achieving them in the real world. We come to realize that the real world is the perfect training ground for us. When we concentrate our focus we will remove obstacles on our journey. This will make us stronger.

Obstacles thus serve to strengthen us. Obstacles make us stronger so that we accomplish more. Obstacles are stepping-stones on our journey. When you encounter an obstacle paint it green in your mind and write the word "GO" on it. Focus your mind on your desirable end result. Feel your burning desire for your outcome. A solution will become apparent to you. NOW take action! Get going! You will become stronger and more capable by filling with, and feeling the energy that you create by taking action now.

Thought is creative. If you ever doubted this then travel to a city. Look around you. Every single thing in the environment there began as a thought in one or another person's mind. Thought is the origin of all manifestation. Energy was then channeled along the lines laid by thought to bring about the desired results. The energy was ready to be channeled. The materials were pre-existing. The only thing truly created was thought and the rest was then channeled and transformed by thought.

The main focus of this book is to explore and affirm the truth that our thoughts are a creative force in our life. A proven method of manifestation is to visualize your goals. Visualization is the process of making the mold, or model, which will serve as the pattern from which your future will emerge. I encourage you to make your pattern clear and beautiful. You are unlimited so you may as well make your pattern grand and wonderful.

Imagine your end result as already existing. Imagine doing what you love to do. Spend time dreaming about your end result so that you can see the picture more and more completely. Clearness and accuracy are obtained only by repeatedly holding the image in your mind. Each time your vision is revisited your image becomes more clear and accurate.

Likewise, the degree of your outward manifestation increases according to your increasing clarity and accuracy. Jim Carey clearly visualized an ideal and this helped him to make it a reality. Carey wrote himself a check for $10 million dollars for his 'acting services', and he carried his check in his wallet until his vision became manifest. You also can hold your ideal firmly and securely in your mind. You also can speed your ideal by making precursory physical changes. You can write yourself a check, or make inspiring notes to yourself on your mirror, or you might want to tape money to your ceiling as a reminder. Use any tools available to help you solidify your vision in your mind so that it emerges firmly and securely in material form.

Continue to hold the details of your vision steadfast in your mind, and as the details become clear in your mind the ways and means for achieving them will also become clear. Create your vision. Make it clear and hold it firmly. Your confident desire for the results will naturally lead to actions and action will develop methods for manifesting your vision.

Other people will become excited by your dream and will want to help you. Your friends will connect to more circumstances and make more resources available to you. As you take more steps you feel more and more powerful energy flowing through you. In the end, one cycle of materialization will have been accomplished and you can prepare for the next round of the cycle of creation.

Seeing the end result clearly and in detail supports your belief in the attainability of your vision. Your belief in the attainability unleashes a burning desire for its fulfillment. Burning desire brings about a demand for results, leading you to action. Action allows the energy to flow transforming materials in the process of manifestation.

The images in your mind are the templates for your creation. Make these templates as ideal as possible. Make your images beautiful and opulent. Give no thought to external conditions as these are easily transformed. Concentrate on the things you desire to create for your self, until they become the entire content of your mind. Think of abundance and contemplate the methods and plans for putting these into operation. The creative power of thought brings about conditions of abundance and opulence for those who entertain thoughts of courage and power.

I encourage you to use only constructive, positive words and images and to express these in their purest form. For example it is much better to say, I love, which conjures only positive energy, rather than I hate, which places the emphasis on the antithesis of what you desire. I love creates that which you desire, whereas the latter allows the negative to occupy your imagination. Likewise, I do not want places the emphasis on that which you do not want! When you phrase your wishes as a double negative you have introduced the negative, perhaps twice. When you notice negative terms creeping into your thoughts then practice rephrasing your statements so that they use only the purest of positive terms.

During constructive imagination you visualize your desired result in its completion as existing in the present. You see your desired result as already done. Your mind naturally desires and pursues desirable things and situations that it knows exist and are obtainable. When you visualize ideals in their full completion you are signaling to your mind that the ideal exists and is worthy of pursuit.

Plant your seed of visualization in your mind and then leave it undisturbed and unperturbed. You would not dig up an actual seed from your garden to ensure that it is germinating; likewise you do not dig up your seed of visualization to examine it or to show everyone around you its state of growth.

Allow your seed to grow with love and concentration and you will see it sprouting sure enough in time. You will do better work than you have ever done before, knowing that your seed is growing and the results you seek are coming closer to you. While enjoying quiet confidence new channels for your fulfillment open up. Stay open and be ready to act when the time comes. Ask a few key questions and await the response.

Now revisit your toplife list knowing that you accomplish anything you set your mind on. Knowing that you can achieve anything or everything on your list, do you feel a pull toward any area of interest? Knowing that you can have anything, what then do you desire? What do you choose to bring into existence? Is it wonderful? If nothing on your toplife list speaks to you as a burning desire, write down something that **DOES** feel wonderful to you. Go ahead, name the most wonderful thing you can imagine and put it on your list.

Hold the ideals that you wish to realize in your minds eye. Keep in mind the next step necessary for its realization. Do this, and you become aware when circumstances are ready for your plans to materialize. The results obtained correspond to the fidelity with which you are able to visualize your ideal. The ideal you hold in your mind predetermines and attracts the conditions necessary for its fulfillment. The quality of your ideal determines the quality of the fulfillment.

Imagination as used herein is different than mere daydreaming. Daydreaming meanders with free association and has very little sense of purpose and direction. Imagination as used herein is focused toward the accomplishment of chosen ideals. Imagination follows the principles we have described and is concentrated until it is a powerful force used for deliberate creation. Imagination is the most productive labor that a human being can perform.

Hold in mind the desired result. Visualize it as complete and already existing. By constant repetition the desired result becomes a part of our selves. Neurons that fire together wire together. By repeating our visualizations we are actually changing ourselves and making ourselves what we desire to be.

The character you desire to embody, and the vision you choose to create for your life, is not a matter of chance but a feat of practice and of continued effort. You make yourself capable and strong as you substitute weak thoughts of ~~fear~~, ~~lack~~ and ~~limitation~~, with thoughts of **courage**, **power**, **self-reliance** and **confidence**.

Focusing on an ideal sometimes awakens negative emotions. What do you do if a negative emotion resists being supplanted by a positive emotion? When you avoid feeling an emotion then you are reacting to it rather than transforming it. We make much better progress when we embrace emotions by feeling them rather than trying to run from them.

When feelings arise then feel them. Encourage the feelings to grow. Shine your love on your emotions even when they are negative.

When you experience and accept your emotions, you often experience an upward progression towards a more positive frame of mind. When one negative emotion is healed it often transforms into another perhaps less negative emotion. As we continue embracing and loving each emotion we almost invariably rise towards enthusiasm, health and vitality.

If you feel sadness, then allow your sadness to fill you. Shine your love on your sadness. Spend some time with it. Your sadness may turn into fear. If you feel fear then embrace it. Feel it. Grow it. Shine your loving acceptance on it. Fear is said to be an acronym for 'False Evidence Appearing Real'. It is also however, 'Faith Ever Available Returning'.

Your fear may turn into pain. You may feel emotionally hurt. Feel the hurt. Console yourself. Love the hurt. The hurt may give way to faith. This is nicer feeling, but do not stop here. Feel the faith. Love the faith. Spend time being in it, but do not make this your final destination. You faith will eventually lead to feelings of enthusiasm about your life, and provide you a wellspring of delicious energy. When this happens you will be at the highest point of your emotional wellness. You will find yourself in a totally positive space, in touch with spirit and tapping into the abundant energy of the universe.

Equally important to making constructive and conscious choices for your thoughts, your words, and your emotions, is to choose to focus on areas where you have an intrinsic interest according to your unique personality. You took the personality probe to find areas of intrinsic interest to you and you captured these areas of interest in your toplife list.

There is little use visualizing selling volumes of insurance contracts when you dislike selling and/or insurance. If you have a passion, or a calling in one or more paths, then it is critical to focus on one of these paths. When you focus on a path for which you have an intrinsic interest, and you see the outcome in detail as already accomplished and believable, then you are able to sustain a growing desire for that outcome. Once you obtain this desire and nurture this desire you will naturally take steps toward its fulfillment.

Remember that you have already seen proof of the power of thought to manifest events that may seem incredible. I have a Masters of Science Degree, and have written books on Quantum Mechanics. I am happy to share with you what the equations of quantum mechanics tell us about physical reality.

The equations of Schrödinger, Dirac, Feynman Diagrams etc., tell us that nature explores ALL the possible ways to accomplish any ONE particular physical event. The probability of occurrence involves a summation of the field strength over all possible paths.

Paths that generate a lot of NEGATIVE interference are SUPPRESSED. The paths that reinforce each other POSITIVELY are ENHANCED becoming more PROBABLE. The physical universe acts as a giant internal consistency calculator. All options are worked through, exactly as if a mind were thinking its way through all the possibilities. The result of all this activity is a single emission and absorption event that is an exchange of energy. All of the emission and absorption events taken together constitute the physical reality we experience through our senses and through our instruments.

The physical world of our senses, and of our equipment, records only the emission and absorption events, but does not record all of the exploration and evaluation of all of the paths that show up in our equations. Our physical senses, and all of our scientific equipment, thus miss almost all of what happens during the course of any physical event.

From the equations of quantum mechanics, we learn that physical reality is a vast possibility-exploring engine whose outcomes favor internal consistency.

Physical reality favors internal consistency. This is an extremely powerful principle. We humans must put this to good use. Positive thought is consistent with positive actions is consistent with positive results. Positive communication attracts positive people and this brings good resources to apply to any positive goal.

Use the principle of consistency as your foundation.

*First find a path that is positive to you. This is a path that is consistent with your personal likes and abilities. You have discovered, through using the personality probe, your own highly desired paths, and you have refined and clarified these by repeated contemplation of your toplife list.

*Next seek consistency between your current situation and your desired result. In other words, see your current reality as being compatible with achieving the results you find most desirable to achieve. This is the same as believing in the outcome.

*Hold your positive goal in mind as already existing. This activates excitory pathways in your brain, which stimulate more activity.

*Refine your desired outcome to make it as ideal and as attractive as possible. Do not limit yourself to what you may now consider realistic. Allow your mind to conjure up what you desire in as pure and wonderful a form as imaginable. Once you believe that you will have what you desire, you sustain a consistent burning desire for it.

*Constructively imagine the fine details of your desired outcome, and then you will envision steps that can be taken to bring you closer to your goal.

*Achieve consistency in your actions so that your actions reinforce and thus progressively increase the likelihood of occurrence of those steps leading to your goal.

Inexorably, you move closer to your desired outcomes, one step after the other, until you achieve them.

Part V

"Follow your bliss." Joseph Campbell

This book has demonstrated to you that the universe is one giant consistency engine and that consistency is thus the master key to obtaining everything you desire in life. The universe is constantly exploring all possible options and selects the results that are most consistent. Wisdom, strength, health, and courage are all harmonious, consistent, conditions and are the result of deliberate construction upon a foundation of consistency that begins with your self-alignment to your own inner nature.

Revisit your toplife list now. Choose one or a combination of areas to focus on. How consistent is your choice, with your own inner being? Is this what you would love to do? **Is this attractive to you?** If not then what is attractive? Write down what is attractive.

If you are having trouble finding something attractive then it is because you are restraining your imagination. Give yourself permission to let go of any criteria limiting you or any other inhibitions.

Think of something that you would really love to do and write it down. Do not limit yourself to what you think is realistic. You will find that reality can be modeled like clay to suit your ideal. You must establish first your ideal. Then you must hold it in your mind.

What would be ideal? What would you love to do? Write that down on your toplife list. Hold this vision of your heart's desire as fulfilled. Picture your self in your new life doing what you love to do.

You now have in your possession the key to all happiness, health and riches. You have the knowledge. When an object or purpose is clearly held in thought, its manifestation, in concrete form, is only a matter of time.

You now see a path that aligns with your innermost desires and abilities. You see this path as achievable and grow a persistent burning desire upholding an unwavering sense of purpose.

You now know that the universe is a colossal consistency engine. All options for all events are explored. Events reinforced by being consistent across all paths become more probable. When you apply the Canduit cycle you believe that your desire has already been fulfilled, thus making the present

condition consistent with fulfillment.
Accomplishment of your desire will then follow.

The Canduit cycle delivers gracefully what others
toil to achieve. Remember to keep a picture of this
cycle clearly in your mind so that you refer to the
process often. Refine the desired result so that it is a
purified and ultimately attractive ideal. Believe in
your ability to realize this ideal. Allow a persistent
burning desire for your ideal to well up inside of
you. Dwell on your ideal and visualize it in ever
increasing detail. You will see actions that can be
taken to bring the realization closer. Take these
actions and thrill in the pursuit like an ardent lover.

Applying the principle of consistency will ensure
that unopposed thought correlates with its object.
Unopposed thought leads to unopposed action,
which in turn leads to inexorable fulfillment. You
are on your path of fulfillment, joy and enthusiasm.

Your ideal is held in mind, sharply in focus, clear
cut and definite. You know that thought is building
for you what you think of and bringing it nearer.

Your ideal held in mind allows you to create your
ideal physical reality, your ideal businesses, your
ideal home, your ideal friends, and your ideal
environment for you to thrive at your highest good.
You keep going forward and upward toward your

most attractive ideal. You have knowledge of your power. You have courage to dare and power to do.

Your independence and self-sufficiency is founded upon your knowledge of the application of the creative power of thought. You adjust yourself to the law of consistency. Consistency with your internal nature supports consistency between your present situation and fulfillment, which provides a foundation for belief engendering a persistent burning desire upholding an unwavering sense of purpose leading to consistent action bringing fulfillment one step at a time. Thus the law of consistency correlates thought with its object and brings forth in the material world the correspondence with the ideals held clearly in your mind.

Think about what you love to do. Love is the feeling that imparts vitality to thought. Love is another word for desire. Thought impregnated with love becomes invincible. The force of love is the creative force behind every manifestation from the attraction of the electron to the atom to everything of which we can conceive in our imagination. The combination of thought and love, forms the irresistible force called the law of consistency.

By repetition of the ideas and tools given to you in this book, and by putting these into practice, you develop the neural circuitry to implement more and more of that which you desire to create in your life. Intention governs attention. Through concentration deep thoughts give rise to forces of high potentiality. Through repose in silence you reach your subconscious mind from which all power is evolved.

You find success and all power within you. You learn to relinquish control so that your subconscious is free to perform its vast and joyous responsibilities. Your subconscious draws on resources much greater than those of your conscious mind and this sets in motion all manner of abilities of which we may be entirely ignorant at a conscious level. In this way you experience the beauty and grandeur of the opportunities that are at your disposal.

The principle of consistency demands that when you deny unsatisfactory conditions by holding the ideal clearly in mind, you redirect the creative power of your thought away from these unsatisfactory conditions. You thus cut the source of negativity at the root. While the negative withers you plant seeds for the positive, which begin to grow. In this way you steer your life from what is less desirable towards your ideal.

The energy that you invested in negative thoughts may take some time to fully dissipate depending on the magnitude of your previous investment. Remember, if moments of impatience arise, to be kind and forgiving to your self. Love overrides all other emotions and brings you back to the place of manifesting your highest good, your ideal self, and your heart's desires.

You will prevail and any unsatisfactory conditions will progressively and surely terminate while being replaced by your ideal. We entertain desirable thoughts to receive desirable conditions. Intently concentrate on your ideal thereby providing the energy and vitality for your ideal to grow. Focus on your ideal. Hold your ideal in your mind and focus only on that.

Growth is obtained through an exchange of the old for the new and better, thus as your life improves it will necessarily change. Be open and willing to receive the changes that will most definitely arise. When you begin a journey towards your ideal life, change comes. Resistance to change is a form of paralysis that is sometimes created to stop the progression to your higher state of being. Love the changes. You let go of the old, let it crumble away, if necessary, to make room for your ideal.

Our ability to let go of what we have now and to welcome what we require for further growth, determines the degree of harmony and happiness we experience. As we reach higher planes of fulfillment and entertain broader visions, our ability to sense the purpose of what we attract becomes greater and we become progressively better at being able to discern what we require to reach our ideal, and how to absorb all that is available to help us reach our goal. With the ideal firmly in our mind, nothing may reach us except what is necessary for our growth and progress.

The law of consistency ensures that what we reap and what we sow are in exact arithmetic balance. We thus gain permanent strength exactly to the extent of the effort we expend to overcome difficulties. When we are in alignment with our internal selves and are burning with desire and unwavering in purpose, what joy we experience in pursuit! What thrill we feel running up the hill! Great is the rapture of the ardent lover in pursuit of his beloved! We thus gain in strength while we thrill in overcoming adversity. The effort expended is exhilarating and contributes to our vitality and zest. In order to possess vitality, thought must be impregnated with love. Love imparts vitality to thought thus allowing it to germinate. We must thus begin by finding what we love and then follow this by doing more of what we love to do. We think only abundant thoughts and express abundance in our lives. This provides the resources to follow our innermost dreams.

For thoughts expressed in words, we make use only of material that has been carefully selected for construction of the ideal. Choose your words with intention to create a solid foundation. The selection of structurally sound words and sentences is the highest form of architecture in civilization and is a passport to our success.

He who is wise enough to understand will recognize that the creative power of thought is an invincible tool that provides mastery over destiny. When we hold the ideal fixed in our mind we receive the results. We thus visualize only that which we wish to have manifested in our lives and exclude all else. This insight is a power that is best developed in silence by repeated concentration. The way to apply this knowledge is by conscious, loving, joyful, effort.

Once you have ignited a burning desire you must be ever more vigilant to maintain your ideal in your mind and maintain your focus so as to keep all else out. Your mind is the garden that produces the fruits of your life and you alone are responsible for keeping the weeds out and for planting and nurturing the appropriate beneficial plants to

produce the fruits of your desire. The light of your
attention is what nourishes your garden. Shine the
light of your attention on the good plants and let the
weeds wither away in darkness.

The predominant characteristic of wealth is
exchange value. The value of wealth is not static but
is experienced when the exchange secures things of
real value whereby our ideals may be realized.
Wealth is simply a means of securing an end. True
success is contingent on a higher ideal than the mere
accumulation of riches and he who aspires to such
success must uphold an ideal for which he is eager
to strive. With such an ideal in mind the ways and
means will always be provided.

We must guard against the mistake of mixing up the
end for the means. You are truly successful as you
hold in your mind a definite fixed purpose, an ideal.
There are three steps to success and they are
idealization, visualization and materialization. You
determine an ideal that is attractive and congruent to
your inner nature. Then you see the fruits of this
ideal as already existing in the world as complete
and in detail. This leads to belief in your outcome
and to a burning desire upholding an unwavering
sense of purpose. The lover then joyously pursues
his beloved with all manner of actions be they
artful, ingenious, resourceful, well planned … as
necessary and sufficient to bring about the

congruency with his ideal. Throughout this process you focus on your ideal and your commitment and unwavering focus is the master cause that sets all the other causes in motion.

We form our own mental images through our own interior processes of thought regardless of the thoughts of others, regardless of exterior conditions, regardless of the environment of any kind, and it is by exercise of this power that we control our destiny, body, mind and emotions. By exercise of this power we take our fate out of the hands of chance and consciously create for ourselves the experiences we desire. We control our thinking and thus control our circumstances, conditions, environment and destiny.

The potency of your thoughts depends on the depth of impression, the clarity of your vision and the boldness of your image. Think of vigor, strength, courage, and determination and these will be the materials used to construct your image. A constructive thought, aligned with what you love to do, will grow, expand and will attract for itself everything resulting in a complete manifestation. Hold your ideal in mind giving no thought to persons, places or things. The environment you inhabit contains everything necessary for your success. The right people and the right things will come at the right time and in the right place. You bring about the realization of any desire when you form a picture of success in your mind by consciously visualizing your desired ideal. Character, ability, achievement, environment and destiny are thus controlled through the power of visualization of the ideal.

We live in a physical universe that explores all paths and selects the most consistent. We must be careful to visualize only those ideals that can exist in such a physical universe. For example, there is little to be gained in visualizing perpetual motion or levitation when we know scientifically that such things cannot exist in our universe. How much more productive it is to focus on areas that are allowed by our physical laws and thus can actually be carried out. The Law of Consistency is real and proven therefore be consistent with your inner nature and with the choices you make manifest in your life.

The mind comes first. Creative thought is the first cause. You are reading this book thus you have both of these attributes. You thus have everything sufficient to create everything else of your choosing. Focus on the cause and you will not be disappointed in the results.

Many think that concentration requires effort or activity. The truth is that it often requires effort to detach from the distractions of everyday life in order to initiate concentration. Once you begin to concentrate the thought takes over. Before you know it you are so engrossed in your subject that your are conscious of nothing else. Such concentration leads to your intuitive perception and immediate insight into the nature of the object concentrated upon. All deep knowledge is a result of concentration of this kind.

Your subconscious mind may be aroused and brought into action in any direction and made to serve any purpose, by concentration. Your subconscious mind unleashes desire and desire arouses the latent facilities of your mind in such a way that difficult problems seem to solve themselves. When the latent powers of our minds are unleashed we experience unbounded self-confidence that allows us to overcome all obstacles until the goal is reached.

You consciously breathe with the intention of living more fully and abundantly with each breath. Supply equals demand. You demand more and as you consciously increase the demand the supply expands accordingly. You come into larger and larger supplies of life, energy and vitality.

Everything held in consciousness for any length of time, when comingled with belief becomes impressed upon our subconscious mind and becomes a pattern which creative energy infuses into our life and environment. The real secret of power is consciousness of power. The more conscious we become of our interconnectedness with the rest of the universe and of the vast capability of our subconscious mind the more conscious we become of opportunity and abundance. At this point whatever we become conscious of becomes manifest in the material world.

The universe is the "One" verse. There is no other verse so we are necessarily one with all else. The ability to eliminate imperfect conditions depends on mental action, therefore the more conscious we are of our unity the greater is our power to control and master every condition within the whole.

You think big thoughts to accomplish great things. The creative energies of the mind find no more difficulty in handling large situations than small ones. Every thought creates impressions in the brain that develop into character, ability and purpose and these determine the experiences we meet in life. Aspire to the highest possible attainments in anything you undertake. Dare to believe in your own ideas. Remember that nature yields to the ideal. Think of the ideal as an already accomplished feat. The yielding to the ideal may not come all at once or on the very first try. Accept intermittent success as preparation for your final victory.

The law of consistency makes no exceptions that favor of any one individual over another. When you understand and realize your unity you will then appear to be favored only because you have found the source of all health, wealth and power. The real secret of power is to become aware of your birthright and to claim it as your own. Become aware of it and then begin using it consciously according to the principles herein. As you become more confident expand your scope by taking on larger and larger enterprises. You will find that the large is not much more difficult than the small.

To create the perfect body, radiating perfect health, visualize the ideal of perfect health and fitness and hold this in your mind whenever you think of yourself. You may even find a photograph of the perfect body and attach a photograph of your own head to it. Put this modified photograph in a prominent place where you will see it often. Every time you see it this will be a prod to your subconscious. The law of consistency will reinforce correspondence between your ideal and outer reality and will sculpt your physical body shape and the internal configuration of your cells to match the ideal that you hold in your mind. You find yourself drawn to the foods sufficient to make the transformation. You will crave exercises as part of the transformation.

The information you need to make the transformation will become available to you. You hold the ideal physical form in your mind and all else sufficient for the transformation is drawn to you.

Find the mental image of your ideal, or an actual picture of your ideal, and secure it within your mind and anywhere in your physical environment to help you in your conscious concentration on your ideal.

Energy flows in the universe. To make room to receive we must give. The more value we give the more value we receive.

The entertainment of positive, constructive and giving thoughts has a far-reaching effect for good. As desire is the great attractive force, which sets the currents of energy flowing, fear is the great obstacle by which the current is stopped or completely reversed. Fear is the opposite of abundance. You easily displace fear by realizing your unity and the awesome magnitude of your power. You focus on courage and on the ideals you wish to achieve and shine the light of your attention on nothing else.

We make money by making friends and we enlarge our circle of friends by helping them prosper. Success is service. We determine the area of service that is most aligned with our inner nature. Service is founded on integrity and justice. A generous thought is filled with strength and vitality. The thoughts enabling the most profound service are clear, decisive, calm, and deliberate, and sustained with a definite purpose in mind.

Revisit your toplife list. What would you love to do? Knowing that success awaits you with absolute certainty, what do you choose? What you desire is yours to have! What do you desire?

Take your best shot. Decide. Make what ever you have chosen as wonderful as it can possibly be. Do not settle for any less than the very best of possibilities. Hold what you desire in your mind as an ideal. Do not limit yourself in any way based on your current situation. Reality will mold as clay to your ideal. Hold your ideal in your mind. See the ideal in detail as already existing and complete. Feel your burning desire. Release your ideal to your subconscious mind by feeling your desire and holding firmly to your image.

Name your ideal, write your ideal on pieces of paper and put these messages to yourself in many locations where you live. Dare to let your ideal form without compromise. Let it take hold deep within your being where the vast powers of your subconscious merge with the infinite resources of the universe.

Allow the roots of your ideal to penetrate within your being and let the energies flow with total acceptance. Allow yourself to have what you desire completely and in full. Allow yourself to have the very best. Let your ideal permeate your being.

Open the channel to facilitate the energy flow through you. You are open and willing to receive. You are worthy of receiving. Feel the warmth of the presence of your ideal within your being. Allow it to be there, to stay there. Allow your ideal to root more and more deeply within you and through you. Open yourself fully to your ideal knowing that it is already yours. You are living your ideal life now and at every moment of your choosing.

If you enjoyed this book then you may check at www.thinkrichenjoyriches.com for periodic updates.

NOTES

This is your area for writing notes. Please make use of it.

Please also fill out your PERSONALITY PROBE FORM and the YOUR TOP LIFE LIST on subsequent pages. There are multiple copies to accommodate multiple people and/or multiple working sessions and refinements.

A.) PERSONALITY PROBE FORM TO FILL OUT

Question	Rating
Q1	
Q2	
Q3	
Q4	
Sum of Ratings =	
Subtract 10 from Sum to Get Result =	
If Result is Negative then you are Extrovert write **E** =>	
If Result is Positive then your are Introvert write **I** =>	
Question	Rating
Q5	
Q6	
Q7	
Q8	
Sum of Ratings =	
Subtract 10 from Sum to Get Result =	
If Result is Negative then you are Intuitive write **N** =>	
If Result is Positive then you are Sensing write **S** =>	
Question	Rating
Q9	
Q10	
Q11	
Q12	
Sum of Ratings =	
Subtract 10 from Sum to Get Result =	
If Result is Negative then you are Feeling write **F** =>	
If Result is Positive then you are Thinking write **T** =>	

Question	Rating
Q13	
Q14	
Q15	
Q16	
Sum of Ratings =	
Subtract 10 from Sum to Get Result =	
If Result is Negative then you are Perceiving write **P** =>	
If Result is Positive then you are Judging write **J** =>	
Question	Rating
Q17	
Q18	
Q19	
Q20	
Sum of Ratings =	
Subtract 10 from Sum to Get Result =	
If Result is Negative then you are Detached write **D** =>	
If Result is Positive then you are Altruistic write **A** =>	
Question	Rating
Q21	
Q22	
Q23	
Q24	
Sum of Ratings =	
Subtract 10 from Sum to Get Result =	
If Result is Negative then you are Open write **O** =>	
If Result is Positive then you are Busy write **B** =>	

B.) PERSONALITY PROBE FORM TO FILL OUT

Question	Rating
Q1	
Q2	
Q3	
Q4	
Sum of Ratings =	
Subtract 10 from Sum to Get Result =	
If Result is Negative then you are Extrovert write **E** =>	
If Result is Positive then your are Introvert write **I** =>	
Question	Rating
Q5	
Q6	
Q7	
Q8	
Sum of Ratings =	
Subtract 10 from Sum to Get Result =	
If Result is Negative then you are Intuitive write **N** =>	
If Result is Positive then you are Sensing write **S** =>	
Question	Rating
Q9	
Q10	
Q11	
Q12	
Sum of Ratings =	
Subtract 10 from Sum to Get Result =	
If Result is Negative then you are Feeling write **F** =>	
If Result is Positive then you are Thinking write **T** =>	

Question	Rating
Q13	
Q14	
Q15	
Q16	
Sum of Ratings =	
Subtract 10 from Sum to Get Result =	
If Result is Negative then you are Perceiving write **P** =>	
If Result is Positive then you are Judging write **J** =>	
Question	Rating
Q17	
Q18	
Q19	
Q20	
Sum of Ratings =	
Subtract 10 from Sum to Get Result =	
If Result is Negative then you are Detached write **D** =>	
If Result is Positive then you are Altruistic write **A** =>	
Question	Rating
Q21	
Q22	
Q23	
Q24	
Sum of Ratings =	
Subtract 10 from Sum to Get Result =	
If Result is Negative then you are Open write **O** =>	
If Result is Positive then you are Busy write **B** =>	

C.) PERSONALITY PROBE FORM TO FILL OUT

Question	Rating
Q1	
Q2	
Q3	
Q4	
Sum of Ratings =	
Subtract 10 from Sum to Get Result =	
If Result is Negative then you are Extrovert write **E** =>	
If Result is Positive then your are Introvert write **I** =>	
Question	Rating
Q5	
Q6	
Q7	
Q8	
Sum of Ratings =	
Subtract 10 from Sum to Get Result =	
If Result is Negative then you are Intuitive write **N** =>	
If Result is Positive then you are Sensing write **S** =>	
Question	Rating
Q9	
Q10	
Q11	
Q12	
Sum of Ratings =	
Subtract 10 from Sum to Get Result =	
If Result is Negative then you are Feeling write **F** =>	
If Result is Positive then you are Thinking write **T** =>	

Question	Rating
Q13	
Q14	
Q15	
Q16	
Sum of Ratings =	
Subtract 10 from Sum to Get Result =	
If Result is Negative then you are Perceiving write **P** =>	
If Result is Positive then you are Judging write **J** =>	
Question	Rating
Q17	
Q18	
Q19	
Q20	
Sum of Ratings =	
Subtract 10 from Sum to Get Result =	
If Result is Negative then you are Detached write **D** =>	
If Result is Positive then you are Altruistic write **A** =>	
Question	Rating
Q21	
Q22	
Q23	
Q24	
Sum of Ratings =	
Subtract 10 from Sum to Get Result =	
If Result is Negative then you are Open write **O** =>	
If Result is Positive then you are Busy write **B** =>	

YOUR TOP LIFE LIST TO FILL OUT AND STUDY

A.) The areas/paths that interest me the most in order of intensity are:
1.
2.
3.
4.
5.
6.

Other things that would be wonderful are:
7.
8.
9.
10.

B.) The areas/paths that interest me the most in order of intensity are:
1.
2.
3.
4.
5.
6.

Other things that would be wonderful are:
7.
8.
9.
10.

YOUR TOP LIFE LIST TO FILL OUT AND STUDY

C.) The areas/paths that interest me the most in order of intensity are:
1.
2.
3.
4.
5.
6.

Other things that would be wonderful are:
7.
8.
9.
10.

D.) The areas/paths that interest me the most in order of intensity are:
1.
2.
3.
4.
5.
6.

Other things that would be wonderful are:
7.
8.
9.
10.

www.ingramcontent.com/pod-product-compliance
Lightning Source LLC
Chambersburg PA
CBHW072209280526
45788CB00002B/947